CFA level

DERIVATI
AND
ALTERNATIVE
INVESTMENT

Complete in less than one week

M. Imran Ahsan

All rights are reserved

Contents

All rights are reserved 1

READING 48: DERIVATIVE MARKETS AND INSTRUMENTS 2

Study session 16 2

READING 49: BASICS OF DERIVATIVE PRICING AND VALUATION 9

Exercise Value of an Option: The exercise value of option affects the price of option. 14

READING 50: INTRODUCTION TO ALTERNATIVE INVESTMENTS 23

READING 48: DERIVATIVE MARKETS AND INSTRUMENTS
Study session 16

LOS 48a: Define a derivative and distinguish between exchange traded and over-the-counter derivatives.

<u>Derivative:</u> Derivative is a security whose value is derived and dependent upon an underlying asset (like commodity, currency or security). Forward contracts, Futures, Swaps and options are derivative contracts.

Exchange traded derivatives: Exchange traded derivative contracts trade on an exchange and they are standardized contracts. These are also backed by a clearing house so the risk of default is minimized. Futures and some options are exchange traded derivatives.

<u>Over the counter derivatives:</u> These are the custom made and negotiated contracts between two parties without involvement of exchange. These contracts are made to match exact risk return requirements. As there is no regulatory body is involved there is a risk of default. Forwards and some options are traded over the counter.

LOS 48b: Contrast forward commitments with contingent claims.

Forward commitment: The commitments on future, forward and swaps are the forward commitments. The forward commitment is the legally binding promise between seller and buyer to transact in future. Forward commitment is an obligation on both parties to carry out a transaction as planned.

Contingent claims: Options and modified swaps are contingent claims because their payouts depend on the happening of an event in future. Once that even happened the option needed to be exercised. In contingent claim the one party (buyer) has right to carry out a transaction (not the obligation) and the other party (the seller or writer of option) has the obligation to carry out a transaction if holder of option want to.

LOS 48c: Define forward contracts, futures contracts, options (calls and puts), swaps, and credit derivatives and compare their basic characteristics.

Derivative contracts can be classified in following types
1. Forward commitments
2. Contingent claims

Forward commitments
Within forward commitments we have forward contracts, future contracts and swaps.

Forward contracts: It is a forward commitment in which two parties are agreed to transact an underlying asset at a future date at a fixed price (decided at current time). This is over the counter contract, means two parties negotiated the contract according to their need (tailored) and there is no involvement of exchange. At the decided date there is risk that one party will not honor its side of contract called default risk. Forward contract is used to remove the uncertainty of price in future. No party pays anything at inception of this contract. If the price of underlying asset increases over the life of contract, the party with right to buy the contract (the party holding long position) has positive value of the contract but the right to sell party (party holding short position) has negative value of the contract. On the other hand if the price of underlying decreases the opposite of above is true.

A forward contract can be settled by delivery of underlying asset or just by exchange of cash. In cash settlement, the difference of exercise and current price is paid to the one party.

At inception of the contract the value of the contract is same for the both of the parties (if we exclude the cost of the contract). Cash settled forward contracts are also called *contracts for difference or non-deliverable forwards (NDFs)*

Future contracts: Future contracts are like forward contracts but they are traded in exchanges and are standardized (not tailor made). It means future contracts involve clearing house, exchanges and regulations. In future contracts daily cash settlement is required for gains and loss at the end of each trading day. These contracts also can be settled in cash or by delivering of underlying assets.

In future contract initial margin is required to be deposited. The accounts of each party is debited or credited as the price moves up or down (called mark to market). With cash settlement, at expiration date the final mark to market is completed. If the deposited amount falls from a certain level the concerned party receives a margin call to deposit more cash. At any point of time the numbers of outstanding contracts are called *open interest*. Some future contracts have price limits called band. If the price hits above or below band the trade stops and restarts if the both parties agrees.

Swaps: A swap is over the counter contract. In swaps two parties agree to exchange cash flows or liabilities. Generally one side cash flow is fixed and other side cash flow is variable. At the settlement date the net amount is paid to the concerned party. There is no payment at the time of inception of swap. The most common type of swap is interest rate swap and credit swaps to hedge (or to speculate) interest rate risk and credit default risks respectively. In credit swap one part gives periodic payments to another party and other party will pay the agreed amount to first party in case of credit default.

Contingent claims

Options, credit derivatives and asset backed securities are contingent claims. In contingent claims the one party (buyer of contract) has right (not the obligation) to carry out a transaction (buying or selling of underlying asset) at predetermined price at expiration of contract. Seller of the contract has obligation (not right) to transact at expiration at predetermined price if buyer uses its right.

Options:
The buyer (or owner) of call option has the right to buy underlying asset at predetermined price (strike or exercise price) for a specific time period (the position is called long call). The buyer or owner of put option has the right to sell the underlying at exercise price in a specific period of time (the position is called long put).
The seller of an option is called option writer. The seller of call option has the obligation to sell the underlying asset at exercise price in or on a specific time period the position is called short call). The seller of put option has the obligation to buy the underlying at exercise price in a specific period of time (short put).
At the inception of option the buyer pays option premium to the option writer. The buyer has no obligation except option premium. This option premium is called option price.
American option can be exercised at any time until expired. The European option can only be exercised at expiration. So the American option has different value than European (at expiration they are same for same underlying).

Credit derivatives: Credit derivatives provide protection to the buyer (or bondholder) against credit default event. Credit default swap (CDS) is a credit derivative which provides insurance against credit default. The buyer of this instrument makes regular payments to the seller. In case of credit default the seller pays the agreed amount to the buyer. If default does not happen the seller does not pay anything. In case of bond the seller can also pay the buyer if the value of bond falls from a certain level.

LOS 48d: Determine the value at expiration and profit from a long or a short position in a call or put option.

Value of long call option: Long call option means buying and holding the call option.
The value of call option at expiry is greater of zero or price of underlying at expiration date minus exercise price.
Value of long call option = max (0, underlying price – exercise price)
Profit of long call option = max (0, underlying price – exercise price) – option premium

Value of long put option: Long put option means buying and holding a put option.
Value of put option is opposite to call option. It is greater of zero or exercise price minus price of underlying at expiration date.

Value of put option = max (0, exercise price - underlying price)
Profit of long put option = max (0, exercise price - underlying price) – option premium

Profits from short call option: It means the investor is selling "the right to buy".

Profit (loss) from short call option = (exercise price - underlying price) + option premium
If the underlying price is lower or equal to the exercise price the short position holder of call option will earn profit otherwise loss.

Profit from short put option: It means investor is selling "the right to sell".

Profit (loss) from short put option = If the underlying price is more than the exercise price then the shot position holder of put option will earn profit, otherwise he would be in loss.

LOS 48e: Describe purposes of, and controversies related to, derivative markets.

Benefits and purposes of derivatives
1. With the help of derivatives the risk can be hedged /transferred to another party even without trading the underlying asset. So derivatives contribute in efficient risk management.
2. The transaction cost with derivatives is lower than trading underlying asset.
3. Derivative markets are more liquid than underlying asset market.
4. Short positions can be taken easily with the help of derivatives.
5. Derivatives contribute in market efficiency with lower transaction cost.
6. They also provide future price information.

Controversies and criticism on derivatives
1. Derivatives can be very risky for less informed investors.
2. Derivatives also attract gambling.
3. Excessive speculation can generate market instability.
4. Derivatives are complex.

LOS 48f: Explain arbitrage and the role it plays in determining prices and promoting market efficiency.

When an asset is priced differently in different markets the market participants buys from low priced market and sell in high priced market and earns riskless return. This action is called arbitrage. Due to arbitrage the prices adjust quickly so the same asset would be priced same.

Law of one price: It states that the arbitrage process brings the price of same or identical assets, equal. Even if two stocks A and B are same regarding future return, they would be priced same. If they are priced different the arbitrageurs will exploit this opportunity and demand and supply will adjust in a way that both stocks will be priced same.

Always remember that the adjusted price does not tell us about fundamentals value of stock. It only tells us relative value of asset with respect to another.

Investment strategy:
If payoffs on a stock are certain, there is no risk (the risk is variation in returns) in investing in that asset or portfolio. That return should be equal to risk free rate of return. If not, arbitrage opportunity emerges. The arbitrageur will borrow with risk free rate of return and buys that stock if the return is higher on that stock. If rate of return is lower for that asset or portfolio than risk free rate of return, then the arbitrageur would short that stock and invest in risk free return and will earn profit.

READING 49: BASICS OF DERIVATIVE PRICING AND VALUATION

LOS 49a: Explain how the concepts of arbitrage, replication, and risk neutrality are used in pricing derivatives.

Arbitrage: When an asset is priced differently in different markets, the market participants buy from low priced market and sell in high priced market and earn riskless return. This action is called arbitrage. Due to arbitrage the prices adjust quickly so the same asset would be priced same. Arbitrage process brings the price of same or identical assets equal which is called law of one price. Sometimes the cost of exploiting this opportunity is higher than the transaction cost. In this case very small price difference may exist.

Replication: Is a process of creation of an asset or portfolio from other assets or derivatives. For example
Long asset + short derivative = risk free asset
In this process we assume no-arbitrage condition because in case of arbitrage opportunity the prices may differ.
By replication investors earn return equal to risk free rate of return in long run. It is like holding a risk free bond.

Risk neutrality: Mostly investors are risk averse. Means they want to minimize risk or will accept risk if it compensate returns. For risk averse investors, every risky security's expected returns (all cash inflows) would be discounted by risk free rate of return plus risk premium to calculate the price of a security.

For investors who are risk neutral the expected future returns (all cash flows) are discounted at risk free rate of return (only) to calculate the price of a security. This is because the risk neutral investor does not differentiate between risk free and risky assets.

LOS 49b: Distinguish between value and price of forward and futures contracts.

At inception of forward and future contracts, the value is zero. As the value (expected future value) of underlying asset changes, the value of contract changes. The value of a contract is what investors determine and willing to trade for. If the value is more (less) than the current market price, the investors will buy (short) the contract.
The price of future or forward contract is fixed which is agreed at the inception of contract.

LOS 49 c: Calculate a forward price of an asset with zero, positive, or negative net cost of carry.

The forward price must be equal to "the spot price of underlying compounded over life of forward contract at risk free rate + future value of carrying cost compounded over the life of contract.

When there is positive carrying cost, then future price is always greater than spot price. In absence of carrying cost the forward price is just the spot price of underlying compounded at risk free rate over the life of forward contract. Again the future price would be higher (but lower than the future price with carrying cost) than spot price. In case of negative carrying cost the future price can be lower than spot price. We can experience negative carrying cost when we have positive cash flows (which are in excess of carrying cost) from the underlying asset (dividends etc).

LOS 49d: Explain how the value and price of a forward contract are determined at expiration, during the life of the contract, and at initiation.

At initiation: At initiation the forward contracts is set in a way so that the value becomes zero for both parties. For example, let's assume net cost and benefit of holding an asset is zero. The only cost of holding that asset is opportunity cost which is risk free rate of return. The future price of that asset must be the current price compounded by risk free rate of return.

During life of contract: During the life of contract (before expiration) the value of forward contract is equal to spot price of underlying asset minus present value of forward price.

At expiration: At expiration the discounting will not take place so the value is same as price.

LOS 49e: Describe monetary and nonmonetary benefits and costs associated with holding the underlying asset and explain how they affect the value and price of a forward contract.

Cost of holding underlying asset affects both price and value of the forward contract. Carrying and opportunity costs affect the holding of underlying asset.

Carrying cost: Carrying or storage and other costs, like insurance costs of holding an asset, affect the decision of investors. Considering only storage cost, the forward price must be equal to "the spot price of underlying compounded over life of forward contract at risk free rate + future value of storage cost compounded over the life of contract. If we hold forward contract instead of underlying asset we can avoid the storage cost. The value of the contract today must be the present value of underlying (discounted) + costs associated with holding that asset (can be discounted if needed).

Opportunity cost: Opportunity cost must also be considered when investing. Opportunity cost is the potential gain from next best alternative which is foregone. It can be risk free rate of return if the contract is risk free.

Convenience yield: This is the main non-monetary benefit of holding an asset in physical form rather than holding a contract. Sometimes it is beneficial to hold underlying asset instead of holding a contract. Holding a good amount of oil can be a good example. There are always chances of a shortage of oil in future and the prices would go up. At that time, convenience yield is the difference between inflamed price and the price you already paid.

LOS 49f: Define a forward rate agreement and describe its uses.

Forward rate agreement (FRA): Forward rate agreement is a derivative contract with interest rate as underlying rather than an underlying asset. The buyer of FRA faces a fixed interest rate (for borrowing or lending) and the seller of the contract will receive the variable rate of interest in future date. The buyer protects himself from the risk of variation in interest rate. At settlement date the difference between the agreed rate and actual rate of interest in paid to concerned party. FRA is over the counter instrument. So it is tailor made. LIBOR rate is most commonly used rate for FRA.

USES: FRAs are used by firms to hedge interest rate risk for borrowing or lending. For example a lending firm will short the FRA.

LOS 49g: Explain why forward and futures prices differ.

Forward contracts have default risk while futures don't. In absence of default risk the prices of future and forwards would be same (if they are same in all other aspects).
If interest rate does not change or is not correlated with future prices then the forwards and futures are priced same (if they are same in all other aspects).
When interest rate and future prices are positively correlated then futures are priced higher than forwards. Because the margin deposited in banks in case of futures would be invested in short term securities and overall yield would be higher. In this case the investors tend to hold futures instead of forwards.
When the interest rate is negatively correlated with future prices then the opposite of above is true. People would hold forward contract instead of futures.
In practice the experts don't price these two differently.

LOS 49h: Explain how swap contracts are similar to but different from a series of forward contracts.

Similarities: Both swaps and forward contracts are over the counter instruments.
In forward contract the one party pays the net amount to another party at settlement date while in a swap one party

gets the fixed amount while the other party receives a series of payments. If we construct many forward contracts for same payment schedule as of swaps, both are equal.

Difference: For a five year swap the contract is made and the terms are fixed at initiation of the contract. For a series of forward contracts for five years each time the parties have to re-negotiate the terms at expiration. The cost of carrying underlying asset (for forward contract) may vary in different time periods. So the prices of forward contract may differ from swap.

LOS 49i: Distinguish between the value and price of swaps.

Pricing of swaps is determined at the initiation of the contract while the value of a swap is the market value during life of swap contract. The swaps are same as series of forward contracts each created at swap price. If the present value of swap is non zero the party who values the swaps more (will receive more cash flows) will pay the other party.

LOS 49j: Explain the exercise value, time value, and moneyness of an option.

Exercise Value of an Option: The exercise value of option affects the price of option.
In American option the holder of option has the right to sell or buy before expiration if the option is `at the money` or `in the money`.

At the money: It means price of underlying asset and strike price are same.
In the money: A call option is in the money for holder of option when the price of underlying asset is higher than strike price. It means the holder can gain by exercising the option and will buy the asset at lower price (at strike price) from option writer and sell it in the market. A put-option is in the money when the strike price is higher than the price of underlying asset.
In European option the holder of option can exercise the option at expiration only.

Time value of an option: More the option has time period more are the chances that the underlying will move in favorable direction. So greater the time horizon of an option, the more it has value.

Moneyness of an option: Moneyness of an option is the relative value of underlying asset with respect to strike price. At the money: It means price of underlying asset and strike price are same.
In the money: A call option is in the money for holder of option when the price of underlying asset is higher than strike price. It means the holder can gain by exercising the option and will buy the asset at lower price (at strike price) from option writer and sell it in the market. A put-option is in the money when the strike price is higher than the price of underlying asset.
Out of money: When an option has no intrinsic value. A call option is out of money if the price of underlying is below than the strike price. A put option is out of money if the price of underlying is higher than strike price.

LOS 49k: Identify the factors that determine the value of an option and explain how each factor affects the value of an option.

Following factors affects the value of an option.

1. **Price of underlying asset:** The price of underlying asset affects the value of an option.
   Call option: The price of underlying has positive relationship with the value of call option. When the price of underlying increases, the value of call option also increases. It means the holder of call option can buy the underlying asset at lower price from writer of option and sell it in the market at higher price and would earn profit.
   Put option: Value of put option has negative relationship with underlying price. When the price of underlying increases, the value of put option decreases.

2. **Time period to expire:**
   Time to expire has also positive effect on value of option. More the time to expire, higher are the chances that the prices will move in favorable direction. This is true for both call and put option.

3. **Risk free rate of return:**
   Call option: The holder of call option has to pay in future. If the risk free rate increases the present value of that payment decreases. So the value of call option increases as the risk free rate of return increases.
   Put option: The holder of put option would receive a payment in future. If risk free rate of return increases the present value of that receipt is less. So the value of put option decreases as the risk free rate of return increases.

4. **Volatility of underlying:**
   Higher volatility in the price of underlying increases the value of call and put options for the holders. Higher volatility means that there are more chances that the option will end in-the-money. If the option goes out-of-money then the total loss to the option holder is premium

paid. If there is no volatility in the underlying then there is no need to get into an option contract.

5. **Carrying cost and benefits of holding the underlying:**
   As carrying cost of an asset increases investors tend to buy call options so the value of call option increases. Same way the increase in carrying cost would reduce the value of put option.
   In opposite of above happens when there are benefits of holding an asset like dividends on stocks or convenience yield the value of call option decreases and value of put option increases. In this case the holding of underlying is more valuable than holding a "right to buy". And holding an asset for "right to sell" has more value.

6. **Exercise price:**
   Higher the exercise price, lesser the value of call option, because the holder of call option has to buy at higher price by using option. Same way higher exercise price increases the value of put option, because the holder of put option has to sell at higher price by using put option.

LOS 49l: Explain put-call parity for European options.

Put-call parity means put and call options has some relationship. Following are some terminologies which will be included in our coming discussion.

<u>Protective put option</u>: It is a strategy in which an investor holds a long position in underlying asset and buys a put option.

Assume the current price of asset is A_0 and the premium paid for buying a put option is P_0. So the invested money is $A_0 + P_0$. S_t is strike price and A_f is future price of that asset.

The holder of this asset and option will earn "0" or $X - A_f$ (if $X > A_f$).

Fiduciary call option: It is just like a call option with one addition. The present value of the future payments at time of expiration is invested now in risk free return account or bond. The holder of this option has following transaction The premium paid on call option is c_0 and buying price of bond; $C_0 + Z/(1+r)^t$. The face value of bond is Z and it must be discounted to get present value.
The put-call parity describes the relationship between protective put and fiduciary call options.

Put-call parity: Protective put option and Fiduciary call option gives us same results (payoffs).
The equation of parity can be described as
$A_0 + P_0 = C_0 + Z/(1+r)^t$

This parity holds for European option because it cannot be exercised before expiry. Same is true at the time of expiry of American options. But during term of American options the valuation may differs so this parity cannot necessarily holds.

LOS 49m: Explain put–call–forward parity for European options.

As we have discussed in previous LOS that protective put is equal to fiduciary call. In this LOS we sate that the fiduciary call must be equal to protective put with forward contract (synthetic put). This relationship is called put-call-forward parity.

Just like put-call parity with a slight change. Assume instead of buying an asset and buying a put option, the investor decides to buy forward contract and a risk free bond with face value is equal to the forward price. This strategy is called synthetic protective put.

The value of synthetic put option at inception is

$P_0 + (F_{ot})/\{(1+r)^t\}$.------------------------(1)

Fiduciary call option: It is just like a call option with one addition. The present value of the future payments at time of expiration is invested now in risk free return account or bond. The holder of this option has following transaction The premium paid on call option is c_0 and buying price of bond;

$C_0 + Z/(1+r)^t$------------------------------(2)

This is the value of Fiduciary call option at inception.

As the payoffs of both above discussed option are same there original investments should also be the same. By equating the equation (1) and equation (2)

$P_0 + (F_{ot})/\{(1+r)^t\} = C_0 + Z/(1+r)^t$
$(F_{ot})/\{(1+r)^t\} = C_0 + Z/\{(1+r)^t\} - P_0$

It says that a synthetic forward consists of a long call, a short put, and a zero-coupon bond with a face value of $Z - F_{ot}$).

LOS 49n: Explain how the value of an option is determined using a one-period binomial model.

Binomial means two, so in binomial model we consider only two expected outcomes. The value of an option depends on the value of underlying. If the price of underlying is greater than exercise price then the payoff for call option is S – X. Where S is price of underlying and X means exercise price. If price is lower than exercise price then the payoff is zero for call option. We can develop the binomial model by taking only these two situations.

It means we let the price of underlying to change in one of the two directions; up and down.

The probability of moving up is q and probability of moving down is 1- q. The up factor is denoted by "u" and down is denoted by "d".

Call option: The current price of underlying of call option is S_0. If it moves up we call it S^+ and the call option is valued at C+ and if it moves down we call is S^- and call option is valued at C-.

We know that

C+ = max 0, (S^+ - X) and
C- = max 0, (S^- - X)

The up and down factors are calculated as

u= S^+/S_0
d= S^- /S_0

So these are two situations in which we can price the option. In this LOS we do not have to calculate but to only explain. The calculation of the value of options is in level II of CFA. Following steps can be remembered in valuation of options;

(Step 1) Calculate the risk neutral probability (π)

$$(\pi) = \frac{1 + r - d}{u - d}$$

r is risk free rate and it would be given
d is down factor

u is up factor

The price of call option at current time (time zero) is

(Step 2) put the value of (π) in following formula

$$c = \frac{\pi c + + (1 - \pi)c-}{1 + r}$$

LOS 49o: Explain under which circumstances the values of European and American options differ.

The holder of American option can exercise his right at any time during the term of option while the holder of European option can only exercise his right at expiration. During the life of an option the value of American option may differ from European option if exercising it gives us positive value. At expiration both option are of same value; that is zero (if out of money or at the money) or S – X (in case of in the money). So the American option has either greater value than European option or they both are same.

In theory the early exercise of American call option is not optimal for call option holder. In this scenario if the underlying asset is not giving us any benefits (i.e. dividends or other benefits) the American and European options are same.

For a call option with underlying asset which pays cash, the value of American option is greater than equivalent European option. The reason is simple. The holder of such option can get dividend on stock if he/she exercises it early.

The minimum value of American put option is greater than European put option. The early exercise would be beneficial if the put-option is deep-in-the-money. The put option with dividends on underlying (or other cash flows) does not encourage early exercise of option. A post dividend (or other cash distribution) fall in price of underlying makes a put-option more valuable and it encourages early exercise.

READING 50: INTRODUCTION TO ALTERNATIVE INVESTMENTS
Study Session 17

LOS 50a: Compare alternative investments with traditional investments.

We can divide investments into two broad categories; Traditional and alternative investments

Traditional investment includes investment in publically traded stocks, bonds and cash.
In alternative investment the investors may invest in derivatives, short selling of securities, commodities, paintings and in other illiquid assets. Most types of real estate investments are considered as alternative investments. Vehicle of alternative investments may include hedge funds, private equities and real estate investments.
Mostly alternative investments are included in portfolio along with traditional investment assets to reduce risk. This is because usually alternative investment instruments have low correlation with traditional investment securities. Alternative investment has higher management fee and incentive for performance (performance fee).

Alternative investment is different from traditional investment on following grounds.
Alternative investment has
- Higher management fee
- Less liquid assets

- Less regulation and transparency
- Difficult to evaluate
- Different legal and taxation issues
- Limited historical data

LOS 50b: Describe hedge funds, private equity, real estate, commodities, infrastructure, and other alternative investments, including, as applicable, strategies, sub-categories, potential benefits and risks, fee structures, and due diligence.

LOS 50e: Describe issues in valuing and calculating returns on hedge funds, private equity, real estate, commodities, and infrastructure

In general there are six categories of alternative investment.

1. **Hedge funds:** Hedge funds are usually limited partnership (investors have limited liability). They are usually highly leveraged, hold long and short positions in equity and derivatives, use derivatives, arbitrage and illiquid assets. Managers of such funds use these strategies to earn gains whereas most of these strategies are not available for traditional managers at least not all of them at a time. They may or may not use hedging techniques.
Hedge funds are actively managed and the managers of these funds use aggressive strategies to earn higher return. Hedge funds always restrict redemption. There is a lock period before which the funds cannot be withdrawn. Funds providers have to give early notice for the funds to be withdrawn. There is always a redemption fee.
Funds of hedge funds hold the equity of many hedge funds.

Hedge funds trade through prime brokers. Prime brokers provide many services to them like custodial, administrative services, money and securities lending along with the trading services.

Strategies: Hedge funds can adopt following strategies; Global macro strategy (use of macroeconomic models), event driven (earning return due to happening of certain events), relative value (arbitrage opportunities), distressed/restructuring (buying the undervalued securities of financially distressed firms or short the overvalued securities) and equity hedging.

Benefits and Risks: Managers of hedge funds are experts and use different strategies to diversify and reduce overall risks. But the element of risk cannot be eliminated and there are risks associated with hedge funds as they are actively managed. Usually the returns of hedge funds are less correlated with other securities but the correlation tends to get higher at time of crisis.

Structure of hedge fund and fee: Hedge funds are also less regulated and less transparent. Hedge funds have two types of fee; management fee and performance fee. The management fee is necessarily to be paid to cover the operational expenditures of fund. It usually ranges from 1 to 4 percent of net assets under management. The performance fee is paid only if the performance exceeds the hurdle rate (the minimum benchmark). The incentive fee can be in between 10 to 50 percent. Some hedge funds use high water mark instead of hurdle rate. In high water mark the losses of previous period are also carried forward to check the performance of the fund.

Hedge Fund Due Diligence: Although it is very difficult to select a good hedge fund or fund of funds because of less transparency and limited disclosures requirement, the following factors should be kept in mind in the process of selection.

- Investment strategy of the fund manager
- Process of investment
- Competitive advantage of fund over others
- Valuation methods in use
- Methods to calculate rate of return
- Management style
- Risks
- Risk management
- Historical achievements and returns
- Reputation of fund and fund manager
- Benchmark used for performance calculation

Hedge fund valuation: The value of a hedge fund is the market value of the securities in portfolio. For liquid securities a conservative approach or average value is used. Conservative approach means we take the market price at which the securities can be immediately sold. For example bind price for buying and ask price for sale. In average approach we average the bind and ask prices. For illiquid securities a reduced price of quoted price is used (for bid and ask) to account for the illiquidity. Some funds use NAV.

2. **Private equity funds:** These funds invest in private companies (not publically traded companies) or in the publically traded companies who need funds to go private. Often leverage buyouts (LBOs) are mostly major part of

private equity fund portfolios. LBOs are the use of borrowed money to purchase shares of established companies. Venture capital investment is also part of these funds. In venture capital the investment is made in new companies who have great potential to grow.

Private equity funds are private investment vehicles which have two types of partners; General partners and limited partners. Strategies of these funds can be LBOs, venture capital, development capital and distresses investment. In venture capital strategy the fund invest in large number of small companies who have the growth potential. In distressed investment the fund invest in companies who are financially distressed and desperately need funds. These companies have strong earning potential in near future.

These funds are limited partnerships like hedge funds. Committed capital is what the investors provide to the fund. Committed capital may not necessarily invested all at a time but may be draw- down over a period of time as the new investable securities are identified and added into portfolio. This drawdown period is on the discretion of manager.

Fee structure: The fee varies from 1 to 3 percent of committed capital. The incentive or performance fee is typically 20 percent of profit. The managers cannot get performance fee until the original capital is returned to the investors. If in start the fund performs extremely good but in later periods the performance is less than previous periods, the incentive fee may goes beyond 20 percent. If as a whole the investors are not getting 80 percent of the total profit "claw back " provision make the manager to return the excessive performance fee.

Private equity exit strategy: Following methods can be used to exit.
- Sell the portfolio to another buyer
- Sell through IPO to the public
- Liquidate

Benefits of investing in private equity fund and risks attached: The empirical data suggests that the overall return is higher for the private equity fund in comparison to private equity investment. The data also suggests that the standard deviation was also higher for these funds. This means the risk is also higher. Carefully selected manager with good past experience can get higher returns with adjusted risk.

Private Equity Company Valuation: The private equity funds can be evaluated by the same manner as we evaluate other companies.
- Comparable approach: The use of T/E ratio and other multipliers.
- Discounted cash flow method: The use of discount rate to calculate present value.
- Asset backed approach: The use of book value, fair market value etc.

Private Equity Due Diligence: While investing in private equity the investor should consider the following factors.
- Usually the private equity investments require high investments. Sometimes the changes in interest rate and market variability reduce the net value of invested funds. The investors should keep in mind what would happen if the fund requires its members to refinance.

- The experience and achievements of manager is also important.
- The valuation models in use
- The fee structure and exit process.

3. **Real estate investment:** Real estate investment includes lands, buildings and other residential, commercial properties and also real estate backed debt like mortgage backed securities (MBS). These also include leveraged ownership of properties, real estate backed loans, and investment in Real estate investment trusts (REITs). Income from real estate can include rental income as well as capital gains. Adding real estate assets in portfolio can reduce the overall risk and inflation hedge (the prices of real estate and rental income increases with rise in inflation).

    Real estate can be divided into following classifications;
- Residential property
- Commercial property
- Loans backed by real estate i.e MBS
- Timberland and farmland

Residential property: It means single family home and it is direct investment in real estate. The buyer of residential property can pay cash for home or can get a loan (mortgage).

Commercial property: Real estate purchased for rental income is called commercial property or commercial real estate. This property can also be purchased with cash or by mortgage. Buying commercial property is also considered as direct investment in real estate. High net worth investors invest in this type of property because they are highly illiquid and complex investments with longer time horizon. Real estate commercial properties can also be held by limited partnership vehicle or real estate investment trusts (REIT). REITs are publically traded (unlike limited partnership) firms who invest in real estate.

Loans backed by real estate: Every residential or commercial property can be purchases (whole or partially) with the help of mortgage (loan). The issuer of mortgage is called lender. The mortgage issuer can sell these mortgages in market or through securitization process can issue another security backed by these mortgages (MBS). Buyers of these securities are considered as indirect investors in real estate.

Timberland and farmland: The income from these properties is in form of timber or agricultural products. The changes in prices of these properties and their products are also a source of income.

Benefits and risks attached to real estate

The performance of real estate investment is measured by appraisal index, repeat sales index and REIT index.

Appraisal index is based on the periodic estimates of property values. The standard deviation of this index is normally lower than indices based in real sales of properties.

Repeat sales index is based on the changing prices of same property sold multiple times. A sample method is used in this index which may or may not be the representative of whole population.

REIT index (Real estate investment trust index) uses the trading prices of shares (just like equity indices). Empirical studies shows that these indices have lower correlation with other global indices (except the REIT index because a crisis hits all the equity in some way or other). However the construction of these indices can also affect the results of lower or higher correlation. One thing can be said for sure; adding real estate in portfolio can significantly lowers the total risk.

Real Estate Investment Due Diligence: Local and international market conditions and interest rate can affect the prices of real estate so one should carefully analyze the market conditions.

Changes in real estate investment regulations and regulations regarding loan acquirement (for mortgages) should also keep in mind. The past experience of managers and their achievements are another factor. Developments of real estate also require permits and zones in which the property is being developed. Availability of long term financing and terms of financing should also be kept in mind.

Real Estate Valuation:
<u>Comparable sales approach:</u> It is based on the recent sales of similar properties. The price can be adjusted with respect to location, age, condition and size of property.
<u>Income approach:</u> It is the present value of all future cash flows from property. It can also be calculated as net operating income (NOI) divided by cap rate (or capitalization rate). Cap rate is discount rate minus growth rate.
<u>Cost approach:</u> It is estimated as the replacement cost of the property at current prices.

The valuation of REITs is same as valuation of any stock, the relative prices P/E ratios etc, present value of future cash flows method and asset based valuation (i.e bok value)

4. **Commodities investment:** Commodities investment includes holding physical commodities like oil, metals and agricultural products as well as owning the contracts related to these commodities like forwards, futures, options, swaps, commodity exchange traded funds, managed future funds, individual managed accounts, Specialized funds in specific commodity sectors and investments in the companies that deal with these commodities. Investment like these is made to get exposure in changing prices of commodities. We have discussed forwards, futures, options, and swaps in derivatives part in detail. Here we will have only short description of these.

   Forwards: These are over the counter and tailor made instruments and can be defined as "obligation of selling or buying the underlying in future date at a specific price".
   Futures: These are also obligation of selling or buying the underlying in future date at a specific price. But futures are traded in a stock exchange and are standardized contracts (not tailor made).
   Options: Options give the right (not obligation) to its holder to buy or sell a commodity (or any other underlying) at a future date at a specific price. Some options are OTC while others are exchanged traded.
   Swaps: Swaps are the contract to exchange of two streams of payments between two parties.
   Commodity exchange traded funds (commodity ETFs): These are the funds that invest in physical commodities or

hold derivatives of the commodities. The investors can buy the equity of these funds.

<u>Managed future funds:</u> These are the private limited partnerships (like hedge funds) to actively manage the investments in derivatives of commodities.

<u>Individual managed accounts:</u> These are just like managed future funds except these are for high net worth investors who want commodity exposure for their own investment goals and needs.

<u>Specialized funds in specific commodity sectors:</u> These are the funds to focus on any specific commodity like oil, gold etc. these funds can be of any structure.

Benefits and risks of commodity investment
<u>Benefits</u>
- Potential hedge against inflation
- Commodities provide different returns than stocks so they diversify the portfolio
- Less correlation with other asset classes

<u>Risks</u>
- Over the time commodities have provided fewer returns as compared with stocks.
- High volatility of prices

Due diligence: The commodities prices depend on the demand and supply. Demand is function of purchasing power, value of commodity to end users and market and economic conditions. The supply is a function of productions cost, storage cost and existing inventory. The supply is also affected by many other factors like production cycle. It means supply cannot be changed immediately after the change in demand because some commodities take much time to produce i.e. oil drilling, agricultural products etc. That's why the supply only changes when the demand changes persistently for long period of time. Supply also changes due to weather conditions (for agri-based commodities), economic events and government policies. Whenever an event happens which reduces the supply, the prices will go up. Anything which causes to increase in supply will bring the prices down. Speculators also affect the prices of commodities. All these factors should be kept in mind before investing in commodities.

Commodity Valuation
We know that
Future price ≈ spot price (1+ risk free rate) + storage cost − convenience yield
This equation must hold; if not the arbitrage opportunity arises.
Convenience yield is the benefits of holding a physical commodity instead of contract. If the convenience yield is very high the future price is less than spot price. This situation is called backwardation. If convenience yield is low or zero then the future price is higher than spot price. This situation is called contango.
Following three returns can be discussed in context to commodity futures.
Roll yield: It is a return that a long position holder investor earns when the future market is in backwardation (positive roll yield).
Collateral yield: The interest earned on margin money (collateral) which is required to enter in future contract.
Change in spot prices: It is a gain from changes in the spot price and tendency of change in future price towards spot price in over the term of contract.

5. **Infrastructure:** Investment in long lived assets of public services like roads, bridges, dams, distribution facilities like electricity and similar projects can be considered as infrastructure investment. Usually these investments are made through buying the bonds or equity of the firms attached to these projects.

    <u>Brownfield investments:</u> Investment in the already constructed or build infrastructure. This type of investment can generate stable cash flows but growth potentials are very limited.

    <u>Greenfield investment:</u> Investment in the infrastructure which is yet to be built and constructed is called Greenfield investment. This type of infrastructure investment can generate lower and highly volatile cash flows but there can be huge growth potential.

    Both of these investments can be leased, sold or hold for cash flows. Infrastructure investment, require more funds, highly illiquid and takes much time to be constructed. The liquid form of infrastructure investment may include mutual funds, private equity funds and stocks of publically traded companies that are backed by infrastructure.

    Benefits
    - Greater diversification
    - After construction or development of infrastructure the operating costs are usually very low

    Risks
    - High construction costs
    - Regularity risk
    - Interest rate risk for borrowing
    - Construction risk
    - Operational risk

6. **Other investments:** Other investment can include buying of art objects like painting, investment in horses, rare automobiles, stamps and other antiques. These types of investment do not generate cash flows until sold. The owner can enjoy the collections only. There are usually high gains on selling. There is high storage and maintenance cost. The market for these types of assets is usually illiquid and expertise is required for investment.

LOS 50c: Describe potential benefits of alternative investments in the context of portfolio management.

Benefits of alternative investment (AI) in context of portfolio management

Alternative investment provides us following benefits;
- Low correlation with stocks and other traditional investment instruments
- AI also provides great deal of diversification
- AI is usually less regulated and less transparent
- Alternative investments have illiquid market so there are good arbitrage opportunities
- Historical data shows higher average return for alternative investment as compared to traditional investment

Historical data for alternative investment is usually not available or hard to collect. The average return is usually calculated by using surviving firms (excluding the failed firms as they are closed and not known to data venders) there is biasness.

LOS 50d: Describe, calculate, and interpret management and incentive fees and net-of-fees returns to hedge funds.

There are two fees in hedge fund; the management fee and performance/incentive fee

The management fee is paid as a percentage of value of assets under management regardless of the performance of the fund. The performance or incentive fee is paid when the fund performed over a bench mark and is applied to profits earned. The profit can be any gain/any gain in excessive of management fee or gain in excess of hurdle rate.
Hurdle rate can be a reference rate plus premium (i.e. LIBOR + 1%). The incentive fee can be calculated as the percentage of profits in excess of hurdle rate or the as a percentage of all profits if the hurdle rate is crossed (later is called soft hurdle rate).

High water mark: This is another fee structure of hedge funds. In this structure the incentive fee can only be paid if the net gains are crossing the hurdle rate. It means the gains which just offset the previous losses cannot be given incentive fee.

Fund of funds charge another fee structure. They charge another management fee and incentive fee (in excess of original management and performance fee).
The management fee can be calculated as beginning-period-value under management of end of period value of assets under management. The incentive fee can be calculated as net of management fee (assets under

management – management fee) or independent of management fee.

LOS 50f: describe risk management of alternative investments.

Each item in alternative investment is unique and its risk management is also different from one and another in at least up to some extent. Following are some measures being used for alternative investment risk management;

Standard deviation: Standard deviation is good measure for the risk but in case of alternative investment is could be misleading. First of all data is usually rare for the AI and the tails of SD are usually fat and negatively skewed because of extreme values. The transactions are infrequent and the sample collection, which will represent the population, is hard. So the estimated could be misleading.

Downside deviation: Downside deviation can be better measure to calculate the risk.

Sharpe ratio: Due to the problems discussed above, the sharpe ratio is upward bias and the beta measure also cannot be trusted.

Value at risk: It could be a better measure to consider. It tells us how much an investment can generate loss.

In addition to above the managerial expertise and strategies of the managerial should also be considered as these are also very important aspects.

The use of derivatives, leverage and currencies risk (in case of foreign investment) should also be considered.

That's all for Derivatives and Alternative investment. Hop you all found it helpful. Do not hesitate to contact me in case of any query at
Ch.imranahsen@gmail.com
Whatsapp: 00923465006818

Printed in Great Britain
by Amazon

56752056R00026